CELEBRATING THE CITY OF ORLANDO

Celebrating the City of Orlando

Walter the Educator

Silent King Books

SILENT KING BOOKS

SKB

Copyright © 2024 by Walter the Educator

All rights reserved. No part of this book may be reproduced in any manner whatsoever without written permission except in the case of brief quotations embodied in critical articles and reviews.

First Printing, 2024

Disclaimer
This book is a literary work; the story is not about specific persons, locations, situations, and/or circumstances unless mentioned in a historical context. Any resemblance to real persons, locations, situations, and/or circumstances is coincidental. This book is for entertainment and informational purposes only. The author and publisher offer this information without warranties expressed or implied. No matter the grounds, neither the author nor the publisher will be accountable for any losses, injuries, or other damages caused by the reader's use of this book. The use of this book acknowledges an understanding and acceptance of this disclaimer.

Celebrating the City of Orlando is a little collectible souvenir book that belongs to the Celebrating Cities Book Series by Walter the Educator. Collect them all and more books at WaltertheEducator.com

USE THE EXTRA SPACE TO TAKE NOTES AND DOCUMENT YOUR MEMORIES

ORLANDO

Orlando, city of dreams, arise,

Celebrating the City of Orlando

In balmy air beneath cerulean skies.

Palm fronds whisper in the gentle breeze,

As sunlight filters through magnolia trees.

In the heart of Florida's emerald expanse,

Where vibrant cultures merge in joyful dance,

Lies a city with a spirit bright and bold,

A story waiting, yet to be told.

Celebrating the City of Orlando

Lake Eola's swan boats glide with grace,

Reflecting towers, a mirrored embrace.

Children's laughter mingles with the sound,

Of street performers' music all around.

Church Street pulses with a vibrant beat,

History and modernity meet.

Cobblestones echo tales of yore,

While neon lights promise so much more.

Universal's realms of cinematic splendor,

Whisk us away to adventures tender.

Harry Potter's world, a spellbinding delight,

Celebrating the City of Orlando

Captivates the soul, day and night.

Disney's magic, a kingdom so grand,

Where dreams awaken at imagination's hand.

Cinderella's castle, a beacon of light,

Guides us through enchantment's endless night.

In the heart of downtown, creativity flows,

Murals and galleries, where art overflows.

Thornton Park's charm, a bohemian retreat,

Celebrating the City of
Orlando

Where the spirit of Orlando finds its beat.

The scent of oranges fills the air,

A citrus legacy, beyond compare.

Groves stretch wide in the golden light,

A tribute to the land's fruitful might.

The pulse of sports beats strong and true,

In stadiums where fans cheer anew.

Magic on the court, Lions on the field,

To the city's teams, loyalty revealed.

Night falls with a tropical embrace,

Stars sparkle in a velvet space.

Bars and clubs ignite the night,

With rhythms that echo pure delight.

From sunrise's kiss to twilight's embrace,

Orlando's beauty sets the pace.

A city alive with spirit and song,

In the hearts of many, it will always belong.

Celebrating the City of Orlando

ABOUT THE CREATOR

Walter the Educator is one of the pseudonyms for Walter Anderson. Formally educated in Chemistry, Business, and Education, he is an educator, an author, a diverse entrepreneur, and he is the son of a disabled war veteran. "Walter the Educator" shares his time between educating and creating. He holds interests and owns several creative projects that entertain, enlighten, enhance, and educate, hoping to inspire and motivate you. Follow, find new works, and stay up to date with
Walter the Educator™ at
WaltertheEducator.com.

www.ingramcontent.com/pod-product-compliance
Lightning Source LLC
LaVergne TN
LVHW012049070526
838201LV00082B/3878